Epicurean Delights

Tastes of Kenya

Epicurean Delights

Tastes of Kenya

Kathy Eldon and Eamon Mullan

Illustrated by Moyra Owens

Kenway Publications

First Published in 1981 by
Kenway Publications Ltd.,
a subsidiary of
East African Educational Publishers Ltd.,
Woodvale Grove/Mpaka Road,
Westlands, Nairobi.
P. O. Box 45314
Nairobi, Kenya.

Reprinted 1981, 1982, 1984, 1992

Graphics and Phototypeset by
Kul Graphics Ltd., P. O. Box 18095, Funzi Road, Nairobi.

Printed by
General Printers Ltd., P. O. Box 18001, Homa bay Road, Nairobi.

About the Authors

Eamon Mullan is a delightfully inventive chef, whose fanciful and delicious recipes turn up on restaurant menus throughout Kenya. His training and experience have been varied, beginning with an apprenticeship with the famous Welcombe Hotel in Stratford-on-Avon in England. He spent time at the prestigious Scottish Gleneagles and Caledonian Hotels, and the Adelphi in Liverpool, before moving to the Negresco in Nice. His continental experience was enhanced by a stay at the Hotel de la Providence in Lourdes and the Frankfurter Hotel in Frankfurt. From there he went to Jamaica's Round Hill Hotel, and then to the Coral Strand Hotel in the Seychelles before he and his wife moved to Kenya's historic New Stanley Hotel. He is now Executive Chef of Block Hotels Kenya, the recipient of many international prizes, and has the honour of being a founder member and current first chairman of the Kenya Cook's Association.

Kathy Eldon is the outspoken food critic and recipe columnist for the *Nation and Sunday Nation* newspapers in Kenya. She is a feature writer for many publications, including *Signature*, the Diner's Club magazine. With her husband, she has written three social history books for Wayland Publishers, one of which, *Kitchens and Cooking*, is the story of eating through the ages. Since arriving in Kenya she has co-authored *Making Music in Kenya*, a Macmillan Education book, and was joint editor for a popular guide, *Nairobi, all you need to know, but don't know who to ask!* She hosted her own television arts and crafts programme in the United States, and has appeared on women's t.v. programmes in Kenya, demonstrating crafts and cooking. She is now travelling throughout the country, compiling the first *Eating Out Guide*, another Kenway Publication, with the willing and able support of her husband and two children.

Contents

Introduction   1

Coastal Buffet   3

Barbecues   17

Elegant Dining   33

Traditional Cooking   47

Curry Lunch   61

Comparative Weights and Measures   74

Index   75

Introduction

Tastes of Kenya can conjure up many images in the minds of those who have eaten in this country. To a Maasai pastoralist, it means meat roasted over an open fire, and a concoction of blood and fermented milk which he carries with him on his travels. To his Kikuyu countryman, it is a hearty diet of meat stews, served with vegetables and greens, and always accompanied by the staple maize porridge known as *ugali*. Further west, the people around Lake Victoria are noted for their fresh fish, as well as the tiny silvery dried fish which they make into a delicious stew and serve with rice.

The Swahili cooks who live along the coast prepare an incredible variety of meals using fish, tropical fruits, coconut milk and exotic spices, many of which reflect the influences of travellers who have touched their shores. Further north in Lamu, visitors always remember the tiny cups of spicy coffee and delicate sweetmeats, clear indications of the Arab influence on that tiny island.

To these traditional foods have been added a wide assortment of tastes from other lands. Following the Portuguese and Arab explorers were other European settlers, each introducing their own unique approach to cooking. The English arrived with roast beef, marmalade and pies; the Germans brought sausages, and the Italians introduced pasta. Each group managed to adapt their own dishes to the ingredients they found in Kenya.

The wave of Indian and Pakistani settlers brought curries, ranging from mild Goan dishes to the hearty Punjabi fare of northern India. In recent years, Kenya has been invaded by thousands of tourists — visitors who come to sample for themselves the pleasures of Kenya's beaches and game parks. To accommodate the new arrivals, hotels and restaurants have sprung up everywhere, each offering a different interpretation of what eating in Kenya is all about. Many tourists are astounded by the high quality of the cuisine they find in the middle of Africa, and many wish to take home recipes which they can use to recreate some of their memorable meals.

Tastes of Kenya contains a variety of

recipes reflecting the diverse groups of people who make Kenya their home. The first chapter, *The Coastal Buffet*, deals with the imaginative use of fish found in coastal cooking, where grilled fish is combined with salads and light desserts to ensure a sumptuous buffet.

Barbecues focuses on meat and chicken, and includes marinades, sauces, special salads and unusual deserts to liven up dinner on a hot evening.

For those who love haute cuisine—*Elegant Dining* features international recipes, some of which have been adapted for ingredients which are plentiful in Kenya, and also are found in good fruit and vegetable shops all over the world.

Traditional Cooking takes a look into the cooking pots of the indigenous people of Kenya, and provides ideas and recipes for anyone wishing to sample the authentic regional tastes found in the country.

Finally, the exotic curries of the different Indian communities are explained in *The Curry Lunch*, a collection of recipes with a distinctly eastern flavour.

The recipes were collected by Eamon Mullan, a chef of international repute, now Executive Chef of the famous old Norfolk Hotel in Nairobi. They have been edited and introduced by Kathy Eldon, writer, restaurant critic, and author of *Kitchens and Cooking* (Wayland Publishers, 1973).

Each recipe has been written with both metric and American measurements, and the book includes detailed instructions for the preparation and serving of the food described.

Coastal Buffet

Coastal Buffet

At any fish market in the coastal city of Mombasa, a multitude of brightly-coloured fish are laid out on wet slabs to be poked and prodded by the fussy cooks who come to buy for the next meal. For generations, the coastal people have been using fish as an important part of their diet, often preparing meals using a combination of ingredients and techniques they learned from the foreign traders and explorers who visited their shores.

Visitors to Kenya will never forget the lavish buffets prepared in the beach hotels, each of which tries to out do the others in displays of marinated fish, samaki curries and lavish shellfish arrangements. Most of the recipes used by the chefs in these grand hotels can easily be adapted to fish found in other parts of the world. The sun-baked feeling of a coastal meal can be re-created anywhere by covering the tables with patterned *kitenge* material of Kenyan striped *kikois*. Serve the food in hand-carved wooden bowls, and use rough banana-fibre place mats, carved napkin rings and a centrepiece of fresh fruit. The ideal accompaniment to the fish is chilled white wine or Kenyan beer.

Soups

Chilled Cucumber Soup
Gazpacho Andalouse
Yoghurt Soup

Fish

Coastal Coconut Prawns
Baked Red Mullet with Honey
Whole Fresh Seafish stuffed with
    Coconut and Ginger
Fillet of Fish with Cashewnuts
Grilled Lobster Negresco
Prawns en Brochette
Lobster Diable

Salads

Fresh Spinach and Cheese Salad
Dilled Prawn Salad
Marinated Green Beans
Fennel and Mushroom Salad
Norfolk Caesar Salad
Hot Rice Salad

Desserts

Pineapples and Kirsch
Malindi Lime Mousse
Tropical Syllabub
Banana Cheese Cake
Taita Fruit Salad with Grand Marnier
    Sauce

Chilled Cucumber Soup

2 large or 3 medium cucumbers
1 medium onion, chopped
1 cup chicken stock
2 tablespoons flour
¼ teaspoon white pepper
½ teaspoon salt
1 clove garlic, crushed
1 cup sour cream
dill weed to garnish

Pare, seed and coarsely chop cucumbers. Place all the ingredients except sour cream and dill weed in a blender and blend until smooth. (If there is no blender, pass through a sieve.) Add sour cream and chill. Sprinkle dill on individual servings.

Serves 4

Gazpacho Andalouse
This chilled soup is a salad in itself

1 kg. (2 lbs) tomatoes, skinned
5 tablespoons spring onions, chopped
6 tablespoons green peppers, chopped
6 tablespoons cucumbers, chopped
1 crushed clove garlic
¾ cup red wine (or substitute tomato juice)
2 tablespoons oil
2 tablespoons white wine vinegar
2 tablespoons lemon juice
2 tablespoons paprika
¼ tablespoon tarragon
1 tablespoon parsley, chopped
dash of Tabasco Sauce

Place all vegetables and seasonings in a large bowl. Season to taste with salt and pepper. Chill for 1½ hours. Serve in bowls, and pass around small wooden bowls with chopped tomatoes, green peppers, chillies, and toasted croutons for each guest to garnish his own gazpacho.

Serves 4

Yoghurt Soup

Prepare the day before to get the best flavour

3 cups yoghurt
½ cup light cream or milk
1 cup water
1 cucumber, peeled and chopped
½ cup raisins
¼ cup green onions, chopped
salt and pepper
chopped parsley, chopped dill
    or paprika for garnish

Mix together all ingredients except the garnish, and refrigerate for a day before serving.

Serves 6-8

Coastal Coconut Prawns

This elegant dish combines coconuts and prawns for an unusual effect

1 coconut
1 ½ kg. (3 lbs) unpeeled prawns
¼ cup chopped onions
⅓ cup sliced mushrooms
150 gms (¼ lb) tomatoes, seeded and
    chopped
¼ cup soy sauce
¼ cup white wine
salt and pepper
2 tablespoons each oil and butter

Split the coconut in half and remove the meat. Cut it into small strips. Place strips in hot oil and butter and saute until golden brown. Remove from the pan and set aside. Peel and wash the prawns. Saute with chopped onions for 3-4 minutes. Add the remaining ingredients and cook for 5 minutes. Season and serve.

Serves 4

Baked Red Mullet with Honey

1 whole red mullet 1 ½ kg. (3 lbs)
½ cup honey
salt, pepper and paprika
oil for basting

Clean the fish. Season with salt, pepper and paprika. Cut tiny slits in the skin and lay the fish in an oiled and heated baking dish. Bake 15-20 minutes in a 350° oven until the flesh is white and flaky. Continually baste the fish with honey.

Serves 3-4

Whole Fresh Seafish Stuffed with Coconut and Ginger

Very easy, very elegant

1 large whole fresh seafish
½ cup grated coconut
2 tablespoons shredded fresh ginger
1 tablespoon chopped tarragon
1 ½ tablespoons sliced onions
6 cloves
½ cup butter
salt and pepper

Clean, gut and scale the fish. Place in a greased roasting tin. Season inside with 2 tablespoons of butter, tarragon and onions. Stud the top of the fish with cloves and cover with grated ginger and coconut. Coat the fish with butter and place in a 375° oven. Bake for approximately 40 minutes.

Serves 4

Fillet of Fish with Cashewnuts

Any good fish will do for this unusual recipe

1 whole fish, 1½ kg (2-3 lbs)
¾ cup crushed cashewnuts
1 egg yolk
butter or oil for basting
juice of 1 lemon
1 tablespoon melted butter
1 tablespoon sherry
2 tablespoons butter for frying.

Season the fish with salt and pepper. Grill, basting well with lemon juice, butter or oil. Mix crushed nuts with egg yolk and melted butter to form a paste. Fry the paste in butter until golden brown. Delglaze the pan with sherry to loosen the nuts. Spread the nuts over the fish and serve very hot with wedges of lemon and sprigs of fresh parsley.

Serves 3-4

Grilled Lobster Negresco

This is a truly delicious dish!

1 lobster
butter for basting
2 tablespoons butter
1 crushed clove of garlic
2 tablespoons chopped onion
½ teaspoon tarragon
1 tablespoon French mustard

Kill the lobster by sticking a knife between the body and shell at the tail. This cuts the spinal cord. Put the lobster on its back. Cut through the length of the body and spread open. Remove the intestinal vein, stomach and soft part near the head. Place on the grill, shell side down. Grill for approximately 10 minutes, basting with melted butter. After 10 minutes, coat the flesh with the mixture of butter, garlic, onion, tarragon and mustard, and grill for another 10 minutes.

Serves 2

Prawns en Brochette

¾ kg (1½ lb) large prawns
6 strips of bacon, cut into squares
1 cup sour cream
2 tablespoons lemon juice
½ teaspoon salt
¼ teaspoon pepper

Thread prawns and bacon on to 6 skewers. Brush with melted butter and grill for 4-6 minutes, basting and turning the skewers occasionally. Remove to heated serving dish and keep warm. In a small saucepan, heat sour cream over low flame. Add lemon juice and any juice saved from the grilled prawns. Cook over low heat for 5 minutes. Season with salt and pepper. Pour sauce over skewers and serve hot.

Serves 6

Lobster Diable

2 live lobsters
1 teaspoon salt
¼ teaspoon black pepper
120 gms (¼ lb) melted butter
1 tablespoon Dijon mustard
½ cup fresh bread crumbs
2 tablespoons butter

Plunge lobsters head first into a pan of boiling salted water. Cover and boil for 5 minutes. Drain and cool. When cool, cut them lengthwise and remove intestinal vein, stomach and soft part near the head. Arrange the lobsters, flesh side up on a baking sheet. Season with salt and pepper. Combine butter and mustard together and pour over the lobsters. Cover with bread crumbs. Dot with butter and bake at 450° for 10 minutes. Serve immediately, garnished with tomato quarters, parsley and lemon wedges.

Serves 4

Fresh Spinach and Cheese Salad
An ideal salad for grilled fish

500 gms (1 lb) fresh spinach
200 gms (½ lb) sliced mushrooms
200 gms (½ lb) farmer cheese
1 red onion, sliced
⅔ cup oil (olive oil preferably)
⅓ cup red wine vinegar
oregano to taste
salt and ground black pepper

Combine spinach, sliced mushrooms, crumbled cheese and sliced onion in a large bowl. Stir together oil, vinegar, salt, pepper and oregano. Pour the dressing over the salad and toss.

Serves 6

Dilled Prawn Salad

1 tablespoon unflavoured gelatine
¾ cup water
1½ cups yoghurt or sour cream
½ cup tomato ketchup
½ teaspoon salt
¼ teaspoon dill weed
2 cups cooked prawns, peeled
cucumber slices to garnish

Soften gelatine in ¼ cup of water. Add remaining ½ cup of water, heated to boiling and stir to dissolve. Blend in yoghurt. ketchup, salt and dill. Chill until syrupy. Stir in the prawns and pour mixture into mold. Chill 3 hours. Unmold just before serving and garnish with cucumbers, lemon and parsley.

Serves 6

Marinated Green Bean Salad
The sour cream and horseradish give this salad a tangy flavour

¾ kg (1½ lbs) fresh French green beans
salt and pepper
2 tablespoons oil
2 tablespoons vinegar
1 onion, sliced
½ cup mayonnaise
½ cup sour cream
1 teaspoon horseradish
1 tablespoon lemon juice
½ teaspoon dry mustard

Simmer the beans until they are just tender. Mix together oil, vinegar, salt and pepper to taste. Marinate the beans and sliced onions in dressing for several hours. Combine the remaining ingredients and stir into the salad.

Serves 4

Fennel and Mushroom Salad

1 medium head fennel
2 medium heads chicory or endive
125 gms (¼ lb) sliced mushrooms
juice of one orange
3 tablespoons corn oil
1 teaspoon castor sugar
salt and ground black pepper
1 tablespoon fresh tarragon

Shred the fennel finely. Shred chicory and place in large bowl with sliced mushrooms. Mix together the remaining ingredients and pour over the vegetables. Spoon into a bowl lined with lettuce or chicory.

Serves 4-6

Norfolk Caesar Salad
A classic Caesar salad

1 large lettuce
4 thick slices of bread
2 tablespoons oil
1 clove garlic, crushed
2 eggs
salt and ground black pepper
juice of 1 lemon
½ cup grated Parmesan cheese
8 anchovy fillets

Remove crusts from bread and cut into ½ inch cubes. Toss them into frying pan in which the garlic and oil are heated. When golden brown, drain the croutons on paper. Place eggs in a pan of boiling water and boil for exactly 40 seconds. Tear lettuce into bite-sized pieces and place in a salad bowl. Season with salt, pepper, oil and lemon juice. Break eggs over lettuce and mix well. Stir in grated cheese, anchovy fillets and croutons. Serve immediately.

Serves 4

Hot Rice Salad
It is the combination of textures which makes this salad special

1 medium onion, chopped
4 tablespoons olive oil
1 green pepper, chopped
4 stalks celery, chopped
2 cups cooked rice
salt and ground black pepper
½ cup salted cashewnuts

Fry finely chopped onions in hot oil for 3 minutes. Add green peppers, celery, cooked rice, seasonings and cashewnuts. Toss the mixture in the pan over a medium fire for 2-3 minutes. Serve immediately.

Serves 4

Pineapples and Kirsch

2 small pineapples
1 cup sugar
1¼ cup pineapple juice
¾ cup water
grated rind and juice of 1 lemon
3 tablespoons kirsch
1¼ cup double cream, whipped

Cut pineapples in half, lengthwise, leaving on the green tops. Remove fruit from the shells. Sprinkle insides of shells with 2 tablespoons of sugar. Chill. In a pan, mash pineapple flesh with a fork. Add pineapple juice, water, the remaining sugar and lemon rind. Bring to a boil and simmer for 5 minutes. Strain and add lemon juice. Freeze for 4 hours. Beat the mixture with a fork. Fold in whipped cream and kirsch. Return to the freezer for another hour. Just before serving, spoon mixture into shells.

Serves 4

Malindi Lime Mousse
A light and refreshing dessert

1 tablespoon unflavoured gelatine
¼ cup cold water
4 egg yolks, lightly beaten
1 cup sugar
½ cup lime juice
½ teaspoon salt
1 tablespoon grated lime rind
6 egg whites
1 cup double cream, whipped
toasted coconut flakes

Sprinkle gelatine over cold water to soften. In the top of a double boiler, mix egg yolks with ½ cup of sugar, lime juice and salt. Cook over simmering water, stirring with a whisk until thickened. Remove from heat. Add gelatine and lime rind, stirring until the gelatine is completely dissolved. Cool. Beat egg whites until stiff. Beat in the remaining sugar. Fold in lime mixture and whipped cream. Pour into an oiled 1½ quart souffle dish which has a foil collar extending above the rim. Chill until set. To serve, remove collar and press toasted coconut around the edge of the mousse.

Serves 6

Tropical Syllabub
Vary the basic syllabub recipe by adding mangos, strawberries, bananas or passion fruit

350 gms (1½ cups) sugar
rind and juice of 3 lemons
1 cup sweet sherry or white wine
¼ cup brandy
3 cups double cream

Mix together sugar, lemon juice, lemon rind, sherry and brandy in a small saucepan. Warm slightly to dissolve the sugar and blend the flavours. Remove from heat and allow to cool. Whip the cream and fold wine into the mixture. Fold together both mixtures. If desired serve in tall glasses. Vary by folding in: 1 cup of mashed strawberries to which ¼ cup sugar has been added, or 3 mashed apple mangos, or the fruit from 8 passion fruits, or 3 mashed bananas. Chill before serving.

Serves 6

Banana Cheese Cake

240 gms (1 cup) sugar
100 gms (½ cup) butter
500 gms (2½ cups) cream cheese
2 eggs
¼ cup brandy
2 mashed bananas

Cream together butter, sugar and cream cheese until fluffy. Mix in eggs, one at a time. Add mashed bananas and brandy. Mix until smooth and light. Pour into a greased 10" round cake pan, and bake in a 325° oven for 25 minutes. When cooked, allow to cool. Remove from cake tin and refrigerate. Garnish with fresh whipped cream and bananas.

Serves 6-8

Taita Fruit Salad with Grand Marnier Sauce

Prepare a fruit salad using seasonal fruits. Serve with chilled Grand Marnier Sauce

Grand Marnier Sauce

4 egg yolks
¾ cups sugar
1 teaspoon lemon juice
dash salt
2 tablespoons flour
¾ cups Grand Marnier
2 cups double cream, whipped

In the top of a double boiler, beat egg yolks. Stir in sugar, lemon juice and salt. Make a paste of flour and ¼ cup of Grand Marnier and add to the egg mixture. Stir in the remaining liqueur. Cook over hot water, stirring constantly until thick. Cool. Whip cream and fold into thickened mixture. Chill. Makes approximately 3 cups of sauce.

Serves 4-6

Barbecues

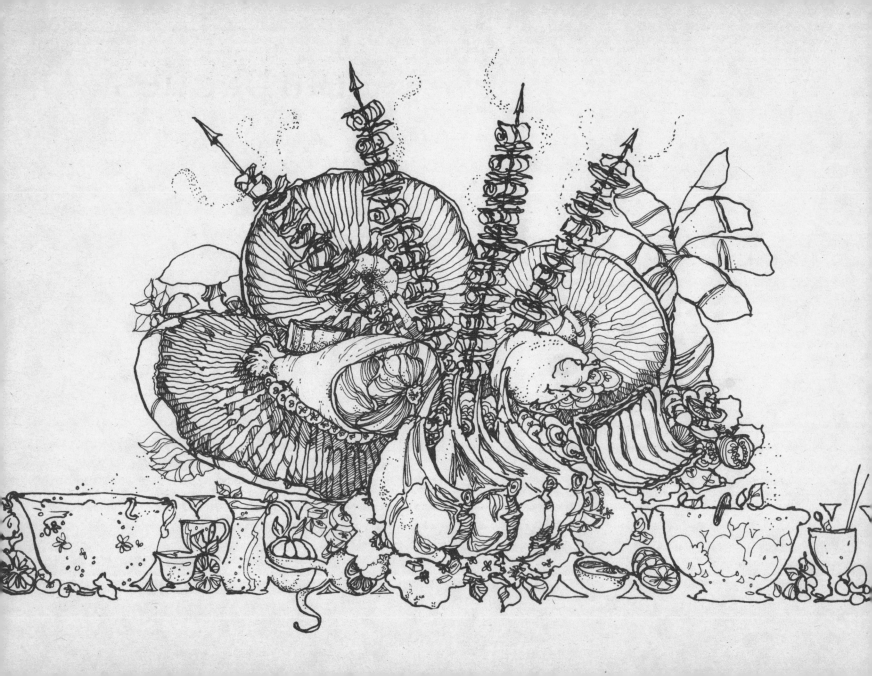

Barbecues

Cooking out of doors is not a new idea in Kenya, where women have traditionally prepared their meals over open fires, balancing clay pots on three flat stones. Recently, however, they have begun using a "jiko," a tiny charcoal cooker hammered out of an old tin. A jiko stands on three short legs and supports a sufuria, a metal pot used for making stews, vegetables or ugali, the maize meal porridge eaten all over Kenya.

The traditional style of roasting or barbecuing meats fits perfectly into modern outdoor living and the casual dining style favoured by many new arrivals from colder countries. Now barbecue lunches often take the place of an old-fashioned Sunday lunch, with guests invited to help cook their own meat over an open grill. A perfect barbecue should include a selection of meat or chicken, several salads or vegetables, and a few light desserts.

Grills

Skewered Chicken with Saffron
Kitale Pork Chops
Mango Stuffed Shoulder of Lamb
Barbecued Spare Ribs
Grilled Laikipia Rump Steak
Molo Lamb **Kebabs** with Paloise Sauce
Barbecued Chicken with Madras Butter

Sauces

Madras Butter
Bearnaise Sauce
Paloise Sauce
Kali Tomato Sauce
Maitre d'Hotel Butter
Aioli
Hollandaise Sauce
Mayonnaise

Accompaniments

Avocado Kaimosi with Hot Dressing
Cucumber Sour Cream Salad
Marinated Tomatoes
Guacamole
Ratatouille
Curried Carrot Courgette Salad

Drinks

Sangria
Nairobi Breeze
Teaplanter's Punch
Keekorok Claret Punch
Toto's Special

Desserts

Superb Strawberry Ice Cream
Lemon Milk Sorbet
Hot Mango Delight
Kenyan Coffee Mousse
Coconut Crust Chocolate Pie

Skewered Chicken with Saffron

The saffron lends a distinctive and exotic flavour to the barbecued chicken

1 roasting chicken
1-2 teaspoons saffron powder
juice of 2 lemons
2 bunches fresh coriander leaves
2 tablespoons grated ginger
1 onion, finely chopped
2 cups sour milk (see guide, page 74)
6 cloves garlic, finely chopped
12 pepper corns
salt and white pepper

Cut the chicken into 12 pieces. Thread meat on to 4 skewers. Place skewers in a flat bottomed dish. Stir together remaining ingredients in a bowl before pouring over chicken. Marinate a day before grilling. Note: turmeric powder can be substituted for saffron.

Serves 4

Kitale Pork Chops

Kenya's Kitale apples give a delicious touch to this easy recipe

6 medium sized pork chops
½ cup chopped onion
2 diced apples
sprig of rosemary
1 cup corn oil
salt and pepper
4 teaspoons Worcestershire sauce

Place pork chops in a flat baking dish. Mix together the remaining ingredients and pour over chops. Marinate a day before grilling.

Serves 6

Mango stuffed Shoulder of Lamb
An unexpected combination of flavours

2 kg (4 lb) shoulder of lamb
50 gm. (2 oz) fresh bread-crumbs
½ teaspoon dried rosemary
1 large mango, diced
½ egg, beaten
salt and ground pepper
oil

Open out boned shoulder of lamb and trim off excess fat. Mix together the remaining ingredients (except oil). Spread on lamb and roll up. Tie tightly with string. Brush with oil and sprinkle with pepper. Spit roast over barbecue for about 1 hour, basting with oil and rosemary.

Serves 6

Barbecued Spare Ribs
Messy, but delicious

3 kgs (6 lbs) meaty spare ribs
1 teaspoon salt
1 teaspoon chilli powder
3 tablespoons brown sugar
¼ cup vinegar
¼ cup Worcestershire sauce
½ teaspoon cumin powder
1 cup tomato ketchup
2 cups water
dash Tabasco or chilli sauce

Put spare ribs in a flat pan. Stir together the remaining ingredients in a saucepan and simmer for 15-20 minutes. Pour over spare ribs and allow to marinate for 12-24 hours. Use as basting sauce when grilling, and serve separately at the table.

Serves 6-8

Grilled Laikipia Rump Steak

Beer enhances the flavour of the steak, and eliminates flames during the grilling

6 rump steaks
1 cup oil
1 medium onion, finely chopped
4 bunches coriander leaves, finely chopped
1 cup beer
4 cloves garlic, chopped
6 peppercorns
1 bay leaf
salt and pepper

Place steaks in flat dish. Mix together remaining ingredients and pour over meat. Marinate for 12-24 hours. Baste with marinade while grilling.

Serves 6

Molo Lamb Kebabs with Paloise Sauce

1½ kg. (3 lb) leg of lamb
1 cup yoghurt
½ cup white wine
½ teaspoon thyme
½ teaspoon grated fresh ginger

Cut lamb into 1 inch cubes, having removed all fat. Combine ingredients in a large bowl, and pour over lamb. Marinate for 12-24 hours, before placing on skewers and grilling. If desired, alternate with onions, tomatoes and green pepper. Serve with Paloise Sauce (see Barbecue sauces)

Serves 4-6

Barbecued Chicken with Madras Butter

1½ kg (3 lbs) chicken
oil, salt and pepper

Cut chicken into portions. Barbecue, basting with oil and seasonings. Just before serving, baste the chicken with Madras butter, and pass the remainder of the butter around with the meat.
(see next page for Madras Butter)

Serves 4-5

Madras Butter

125 gms (½ cup) butter
2½ teaspoons mango chutney
juice of ½ lemon
pinch cayenne pepper

Mix the butter and chutney together. Add lemon juice and cayenne pepper. Roll the butter in foil and refrigerate until required.

Bearnaise Sauce

3 tablespoons wine or tarragon vinegar
3 tablespoons chopped parsley
3 tablespoons chopped tarragon
2 egg yolks
1 tablespoon hot water
140 gms (¾ cup) butter
Juice of 1 lemon
cayenne pepper and salt

Boil the finely chopped herbs with vinegar in a small saucepan until the vinegar is reduced to 3 tablespoons. Remove from heat and whisk in egg yolks and hot water. Place the pan over simmering water and slowly add melted butter, whisking all the time. Season with lemon juice, cayenne pepper and salt. Serve immediately, or keep hot over a double boiler.

Paloise Sauce

Use ingredients for Bearnaise Sauce above.

This sauce is made exactly like Bearnaise sauce, except the tarragon is replaced by 3 tablespoons of chopped mint.

Kali Tomato Sauce
Spicy tomato sauce

1 onion, chopped
2 tablespoons butter
1 chopped red pepper
1 chopped green pepper
1 clove garlic, minced
2 tomatoes, peeled and chopped
1-3 chillies, chopped and seeded
1 teaspoon Worcestershire sauce
salt

Cook together all ingredients except the Worcestershire sauce for 15 minutes. Add sauce and cook for another 15 minutes. Serve hot or cold.

Maitre d'Hotel Butter

½ cup butter
½ teaspoon salt
⅛ teaspoon pepper
2 tablespoons finely chopped parsley
1 tablespoon lemon juice

Cream butter and add seasonings. Beat in lemon juice slowly. Vary the butter by adding 2 teaspoons of mixed herbs or crushed clove of garlic. Shape into long roll and chill. Slice before serving on grilled steaks or chops.

Aioli
A superb garlic mayonnaise

8 cloves garlic
1 egg yolk
¼ teaspoon salt
pepper
1 cup oil
juice of 1 lemon

Mash garlic and mix with egg, salt and pepper in a small bowl. Stir a little oil in drop by drop. Gradually add the remaining oil and stir in lemon juice.

Hollandaise
The perfect sauce

3 egg yolks
¼ cup water or white wine
2 tablespoons lemon juice
125 gms (½ cup) butter, melted
pinch of cayenne pepper

Place egg yolks in the top of a double boiler. Beat them with water or wine until they are creamy. Beat in half the lemon juice. Beat mixture together until egg yolks begin to thicken. Slowly add melted butter, beating all the time. Beat in all the butter and season to taste with salt, cayenne and additional lemon juice.

Makes 1 cup.

Mayonnaise
Vary by adding chutney, curry powder or herbs

1 egg yolk at room temperature
½ teaspoon mustard
½ teaspoon sugar
½ teaspoon salt
dash cayenne pepper
¾ cup oil
1 tablespoon lemon juice

Mix egg yolk and dry ingredients together in a small bowl. Beat in oil, adding it a drop at a time until the mayonnaise begins to thicken. Then dribble oil in, beating all the time. Stir in lemon juice.

Makes 1 cup

Avocado Kaimosi with Hot Dressing

2 tablespoons sugar
2 tablespoons water
2 tablespoons vinegar
2 tablespoons ketchup
2 tablespoons butter
salt and pepper
2 ripe avocados, halved and pits removed
6 slices cooked bacon, crumbled.

Heat sugar and water in a small saucepan until the sugar dissolves. Add vinegar, ketchup, butter, salt and pepper. Simmer over low heat for 15-20 minutes. Pour dressing into avocados. Sprinkle bacon on top.

Serves 4

Cucumber Sour Cream Salad

1 cup sour cream
3 tablespoons grated onion
2 tablespoons vinegar or lemon juice
1 tablespoon sugar
1½ teaspoon salt
4½ cups thinly sliced, peeled cucumbers

Blend together ingredients. Chill for at least 2 hours. Vary by adding 1-2 teaspoons chopped coriander leaves, chopped mint leaves or garlic and dill weed.

Serves 4-6

Marinated Tomatoes

3 tomatoes, sliced
1 onion, sliced
1 cucumber, peeled and sliced
1 green pepper, sliced
½ cup vinegar
2 tablespoons red wine
2 tablespoons sugar
¼ teaspoon salt
¼ teaspoon basil
pepper to taste

Place sliced vegetables in a bowl. Combine the remaining ingredients and pour over vegetables. Cover and allow to marinate for several hours in the refrigerator.

Serves 4

Guacamole

Although guacamole originated in Spain, it is ideally suited to Kenyan ingredients

4-5 ripe avocados
¼ cup lemon juice
¼ cup minced onions
¼ cup chopped fresh coriander leaves
   (optional)
2 chopped tomatoes
chopped green chillies to taste
salt and ground black pepper
¼ cup chopped green pepper (optional)

Peel the avocados and mash them in a bowl. Add lemon juice, coriander and seasonings. Fold in tomatoes, chillies and green peppers if desired. This makes an excellent dip, served with raw vegetables or crackers.

Ratatouille

Serve hot or cold for a perfect accompaniment to simple grilled meats

2 small aubergine (eggplants) diced
6 tomatoes, peeled, seeded and chopped
4 green peppers, seeded, and chopped
4 courgettes (zucchini) diced
2 onions, sliced
5 tablespoons oil (olive oil preferably)
salt and ground black pepper
½ cup water
crushed clove of garlic
1 teaspoon each basil, oregano and thyme
if desired

Combine the vegetables in a large pan. Add the remaining ingredients and simmer over low heat until the vegetables are tender. Serve immediately, or allow to cool.

Serves 8-10

urried Carrot Courgette Salad

2 courgettes, (zucchini) peeled
2 carrots, peeled
3 spring onions, chopped
salt and ground black pepper

Curry Dressing

2 tablespoons lemon juice
½ cup oil
⅛-¼ teaspoon curry powder
salt and ground black pepper

Slice or grate courgettes and carrots into a bowl. Add chopped green onions, including some of the green tops. Toss with curry dressing. Add salt and pepper to taste. Chill. To make the dressing, combine oil and seasonings in a small bowl.

Serves 4

Sangria

This Spanish cooler is an excellent way to stretch wine on a hot day

2 litres (1 gallon) water
2 cups sugar
6 oranges, peeled and sliced
4 lemons
2 bottles red wine
ice

Combine water and sugar in a large pan and heat until the sugar is dissolved. Add sliced fruit and let stand at room temperature for 4 hours. Add wine just before serving in tall glasses, poured over plenty of ice.

Nairobi Breeze

1 part lime juice
2 parts pineapple juice
1 part cointreau
1 part light rum
orange soda

Place all ingredients in a glass. Fill with crushed ice and add sparkling orange soda to the top. Decorate with a slice of orange and a cherry.

Teaplanter's Punch

3 ice cubes
1 dash bitters
juice of ½ lemon and ⅓ orange
1 teaspoon grenadine
1 glass rum
a touch of soda water

Combine ingredients in a tall glass.

Keekorok Claret Punch

3 oz. claret
juice of ½ lemon
2 dashes Curacao
1 teaspoon sugar
ginger ale

Combine the ingredients in a tall glass and top up with dry ginger ale. Dress with crushed ice, chopped pineapple and oranges.

Toto Special

⅓ lemon juice
⅓ orange juice
⅓ pineapple juice

Shake well and strain into a glass over ice cubes.

Superb Strawberry Ice Cream

The addition of sour cream and lemon juice makes this ice cream exceptionally good

1 box strawberries
¼ cup sugar
1 cup sour cream
1 cup milk
1½ cups sugar (or to taste)
1 well beaten egg
¼ cup lemon juice

Wash and top strawberries. Slightly crush in a bowl and add ¼ cup of sugar. Let stand for ½ hour to draw out the juices. Combine sour cream, milk and sugar. Add the egg, juice and strawberries and stir together well. Refrigerate 1-2 hours until slushy. Break up and beat. Re-freeze until solid.
Serves 4-6

Lemon Milk Sorbet

1 cup sugar
juice of 3 lemons
grated rind of 1 lemon
4 cups of milk

Combine the first three ingredients, stirring until the sugar dissolves. Add the milk and beat well. Pour into large dish and freeze until slushy. Remove and beat. Re-freeze. About 15 minutes before serving, remove from the freezer to allow the ice cream to melt slightly.

Serves 6

Hot Mango Delight

Fruit Filling

4½ cups sliced fresh mangos
240 grams (1 cup) sugar
1 tablespoon cornflour (cornstarch)
¼ teaspoon almond extract
1 tablespoon lemon juice
2 teaspoons grated lemon rind

Shortcake

140 grams (1 cup) flour
120 grams (½ cup) sugar
1 teaspoon baking powder
¼ teaspoon salt
1 egg, beaten
¾ cup sour cream
2 tablespoons butter, melted
cream or ice cream

Arrange mangos in a greased 9" x 9" baking dish. Combine sugar, cornstarch, extract, juice and rind, and sprinkle on mangos. Heat in the oven (375°) while preparing shortcake. Sift together flour, sugar, baking powder and salt. Combine egg, sour cream and butter; blend well into flour mixture. Drop by spoonfuls on to fruit. Bake 30-40 minutes. Serve hot with whipped cream or ice cream.

Serves 6-8

Kenyan Coffee Mousse

Add a few tablespoons of Mt. Kenya liqueur or any coffee liqueur to make this mousse even more delicious

2 packets unflavoured gelatine
6 tablespoons cold water
2 cups hot, strong coffee
180 gms (¾ cup) sugar
pinch of salt
1 cup double cream
1 teaspoon vanilla
whipped cream for garnish

Soften gelatine in cold water. Add coffee and stir until the gelatine is dissolved. Add sugar and salt. Cool. When gelatine mixture is firm, whip cream until quite stiff and add vanilla. Whip gelatine mixture until soft. (Add liqueur if desired). Beat in whipped cream and blend well. Pour into individual serving dishes or a large mold. Chill. Unmold and top with whipped cream and grated chocolate if desired.

Serves 8

Coconut Crust Chocolate Pie

Wickedly delicious

2 tablespoons butter, softened
1½ cups shredded coconut
160 grams (6 oz.) dark chocolate (or chocolate chips)
3 tablespoons milk
4 tablespoons sugar
4 eggs, separated
1 teaspoon vanilla
1 cup double cream, whipped

Preheat oven to 350°
Spread a 9" pie pan with butter. Press coconut into butter. Bake 12 minutes. Cool. Melt chocolate, milk and sugar. Cool thoroughly. Beat in egg yolks and vanilla. Beat egg whites until stiff and fold into chocolate mixture. Pour into pie shell and top with whipped cream.

Serves 6

Elegant Dining

Elegant Dining

There is something rather incongruous about the five-course meals served by lodges in the middle of the bush. White-coated waiters pass the food with impeccable style, permitting each diner to select from a choice of soups, fish, meat, vegetables and desserts. Dinner is usually rounded off by a sampling of Kenyan cheeses and sated guests finally retire to the glassed-in viewing areas to sip Kenyan coffee and liqueurs while watching the animals in the wild, miles from civilization.

As Kenya is now the centre of tourism for East Africa, many thousands of visitors are arriving in the country each year, ready to enjoy the varied pleasures of the beaches and game parks. Most are surprised to discover how high the standard of cuisine is in the hotels, lodges and private homes of Kenya, where the tradition of elegant dining lives on. The discriminating diner will find exquisite preparation of food, attentive service, excellent wine and cuisine which reflects the best of international cooking. Most take advantage of the excellent fish, fruits, vegetables and dairy products which are abundant in this country, but it is the way in which the ingredients are combined which makes the food special—haute cuisine with a Kenyan flair.

The recipes in this section can be combined to create an elegant three-course meal which can be made anywhere in the world.

Les Hors d'Oueures

L'Avocat à la Façon du Chef
Les Mangues aux Crevettes Rosés
Les Crevettes au Beurre Froid
Le Melon en Surprise
La Mousse de Voille de Poison Fumé

Les Entrées

Le Filet de Porc Naivasha
Le Canard Rôti aux Mangues
La Gourmandise Brillat Savarin
La Tourelle de Tout Saisons
Le Carré d'agneau Rôti Provencal

Les Légumes

Les Pommes Caroline
Les Épinards à la Crême
Le Mange tout au Beurre
Le Broccoli Polonaise
Les Choux de Bruxelles sautés au lard

Les Desserts

Le Soufflé au Chocolat et Noix de Coco
La Mousse au Moka
La Mangue Flambé à la Sinbad
La Délice aux Fraises
Les Oranges en Glace à la Façon du Chef

L'Avocat à la Façon du Chef
Avocado-Chef's Style

2 whole avocados
300 gms (8 oz.) smoked sailfish
(Smoked salmon or smoked tuna fish can
be substituted for sailfish if necessary)
1 cup Hollandaise sauce (see Barbecue
  sauces)
¾ cup Parmesan cheese

Slice the avocados. Place into an earthen-ware dish. Cover avocados with sliced smoked sailfish. Coat with Hollandaise sauce and sprinkle with Parmesan cheese. Place under grill until golden brown. Serve immediately.

Serves 4

Les Mangues aux Crevettes Rosés
Mangos with Spicy Prawns

600 gms (3 cups) uncooked prawns
2 whole mangos
1 cup cocktail sauce (see recipe below)
parsley and lemon for garnish
juice of 1 lemon

Cocktail Sauce

2 tablespoons ketchup
3 cups whipped cream
½ cup chopped apple
1 tablespoon horseradish

Cut the mangos into halves and remove stone. Drop prawns into boiling salted water with juice of one lemon and boil for five minutes. Remove the prawns, cool and peel. Mix the prawns with the cocktail sauce and place them in the centre of each mango half. Garnish with parsley and lemon wedges.

Add all ingredients to basic mayonnaise sauce (see page 25)

Serves 4

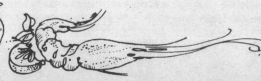

Les Crevettes au Beurre Froid
Prawns in Cold Butter

350 gms (¾ cup) peeled cooked prawns
juice of 1 lemon
cayenne pepper
salt and ground black pepper
¼ kg (8 oz.) butter

Saute the prawns in 2 tablespoons of the butter. Season with salt, cayenne pepper, ground black pepper and lemon juice. Remove from pan and allow to cool. Cream the remaining butter until soft, and mix in prawns. Place in small ramekin dishes and refrigerate for 3 hours before serving. Pass around brown bread and lemon wedges.

Serves 4

Le Melon en Surprise
Melon with Sour Cream and Honey

2 small cantaloupe
4 tablespoons sour cream
4 tablespoons honey
1 teaspoon grated fresh ginger

Cut melons into halves and remove the seeds. Finely grate the ginger and add to the sour cream and honey. Spoon the mixture into the melon halves and chill for one hour before serving.

Serves 4

La Mousse de Voille de Poisson Fume
Smoked Sailfish Mousse

600 gms (1¼ lb) smoked sailfish
   or smoked tunafish
1½ tablespoons chopped chives
1 lemon
cayenne pepper
salt and pepper
1½ dl (¾ cup) double cream
3 egg whites

Mince the smoked sailfish. Add chopped chives, cayenne pepper, lemon juice, salt and pepper. Whip the cream. Separately whip the egg whites until stiff. Gently fold egg whites and cream into the mousse. Place in mold. Allow to set in refrigerator for 2 hours.

Serves 6

Le Filet de Porc Naivasha
Naivasha Pork Fillet

1 kilo (2 lbs) pork fillet
2 tablespoons oil
½ cup butter
1 teaspoon crushed, chopped garlic
sprig of fresh rosemary
1 tablespoon paprika
2 apples, sliced
6 guavas, diced
3 dl (¾ cup) fresh cream
Juice of one lemon
salt and pepper

Cut pork fillet into pieces approx 1¼ inches thick. Heat 2 tablespoons oil in a heavy frying pan and cook the fillets very quickly. Place them in a large baking dish, and keep warm in the oven at a very low heat. Melt butter in a frying pan. Add garlic, rosemary and paprika and stir for 2 minutes. Add sliced apples and guavas. Cook for 3 minutes before adding the cream. Stir in the lemon juice, and simmer until the liquid is reduced by ½. Season to taste. Place the fillets on a platter and coat with sauce. Serve immediately.

Serves 6-8

Le Canard Rôti aux Mangues
Roast Duckling with Mangos

1 duckling (1½ kg or 3 lbs)
½ cup sugar
½ cup vinegar
½ cup mango juice
2½ cups brown sauce (see Carré
   d'Agneau Rôti Provençal page 41)
2 mangos, chopped
salt and pepper

Roast the duck in 375° oven for 1 hour and 15 minutes. Boil sugar and vinegar together in saucepan, constantly scraping edges of pan. When the sugar begins to caramelize, add mango juice. Add brown sauce and simmer 20 minutes. Strain the juice and add mangos. Cut the duck into 6 portions and pour the sauce over the pieces before serving.

Serves 3-4

La Gourmandise Brillat Savarin
Escalopes of Veal in Pancakes with Parmesan Cheese

8·80 gms (3½ oz) veal escalopes
8 crêpes
¼ cup butter
2 tablespoons white wine
80 gms (4 tablespoons) Parmesan cheese
1 cup double cream

Saute the escalopes in a frying pan in the hot butter. Deglaze the pan with white wine. Add the cream and boil to reduce the liquid to ¾ cup. Fold crêpes around escalopes. Place in greased fireproof dish and cover with sauce. Sprinkle with Parmesan cheese and brown under the grill.

Crêpes

300 gms (2 cups) flour
1 egg
2 egg yolks
2 cups milk
oil to fry pancakes
salt and pepper

Whisk together all ingredients except milk. When smooth, add the milk. Heat the oil to coat pan. Pour in the batter and cook until lightly coloured. Turn over and cook the other side.

Serves 4

La Tourelle de Toutes Saisons
Fillet of All Seasons

3 tablespoons butter
¾ cup sliced green peppers
1 tablespoon chopped onions
1 cup mushrooms, sliced
2½ cups Hollandaise Sauce (see page 25)
1 kilo (2 lbs) beef fillet, sliced into 12 thin
  pieces
12 crêpes (see Gourmandaise Brillat
  Savarin recipe)

Saute the green peppers and the onions together in a frying pan with 2 tablespoons of butter until tender. In a different pan saute the sliced mushrooms with 1 tablespoon of butter for 3 minutes. Drain off juice from the mushrooms and add it to the Hollandaise sauce. Grill or quickly saute the fillets to individual taste. Have ready 12 crêpes each approximately 2 inches in diameter. Layer the crêpes alternating fillet, vegetable, crêpe and fillet, ending with a crêpe. Coat the crêpes with Hollandaise sauce and glaze under a grill, or bake in 350° oven until golden brown and bubbly.

Serves 4

Le Carré d'agneau Rôti Provençal
Saddle of Lamb Provencale

1 loin of lamb, approximately 1.2 kg
    (2¼ lbs)
¾ cup white wine
2 cups brown sauce
4 tablespoon chopped parsley
4 tomatoes
1 teaspoon thyme
5 tablespoons chopped onions
1 clove garlic, chopped
200 gms (2 cups) breadcrumbs
4 teaspoons French mustard

Roast the lamb at 325°, allowing 25-35 minutes per pound, depending upon how pink you wish it to be. Remove to platter. Deglaze the roasting pan with white wine. Boil the juices until reduced to ½ Pour in brown sauce and reduce to ½. Add the tomatoes, chopped parsley, thyme, onions, garlic and breadcrumbs. Smear the lamb with French mustard and coat with bread-crumb mixture. Brown under the grill, and serve with remaining sauce.

Serves 4-6

Quick Brown Sauce

250 grams (½ lb) bones of beef, chopped
250 grams (½ lb) shin beef, cubed
4 fresh tomatoes
handful of mushroom stalks
¼ cup fat or lard
¾ cup each of chopped
onions, celery and carrots
1 bay leaf
2 strips of bacon (optional)

Saute the bones and beef using the fat in a large pan until browned. Mix in remaining ingredients and pour 8 cups of water over the bones. Bring to a boil, skim off foam and simmer for 3 hours. You may need to add more liquid. After 3 hours, strain the stock. You can thicken it by adding ¼ cup of corn-flour stirred into ½ cup cold water, and mix together gradually until the desired thick-ness is obtained.

Les Pommes Caroline
Potatoes with Chives and Tarragon

8 medium potatoes
2 tablespoons chives
60 gms (3 tablespoons) butter
2 tablespoons dried crushed tarragon
salt and pepper to taste

Peel the potatoes. Cut into pieces, approximately 1" by 1½". Bring the potatoes to a boil in salted water. Remove when soft and place in baking dish with melted butter, chives and tarragon. Cover with greaseproof paper and bake in 350° oven until soft, about 45 minutes.
Serves 8

Les Épinards à la Crême
Spinach with Fresh Cream

½ kg (1 lb) fresh spinach
30 gms (2 tablespoons) butter
3 tablespoons fresh double cream
salt and pepper

Remove stalks from spinach and wash well. Place in a saucepan with ½ cup of boiling water and the butter. Season to taste. Cover the pan and cook over low heat for 5 minutes. Drain and chop finely. Place in sauté pan, add cream and mix well.
Serves 4

Le Mange tout au Beurre
Baby pea-pods in butter

½ kg (1 lb) mange tout
30 gms (2 tablespoons) butter
1 medium onion, chopped
salt and pepper

Top and tail the mange tout and remove strings. Wash and place in a saucepan filled with salted boiling water. Cook for 5 minutes. Remove from the pan and saute in a frying pan with melted butter and chopped onions. Season to taste. Do not overcook.
Serves 4

Le Broccoli Polonaise
Broccoli with Hard-Boiled Eggs

½ kg (1 lb) broccoli
1 hard-boiled egg, chopped
½ cup toasted bread-crumbs
chopped parsley for garnish

Wash broccoli well. Cook in boiling salted water until tender. Just before serving, sprinkle with hard boiled egg, toasted bread-crumbs and chopped parsley.

Serves 4-6

Les Choux de Bruxelles sautés au lard
Brussels Sprouts sauteed with Bacon and Onions

½ kg (1 lb) Brussels Sprouts
1 chopped onion
2 pieces bacon

Wash the sprouts. Trim by removing outer leaves and make an incision in the base of each sprout to allow for quick cooking. Boil in salted water until tender. Fry the bacon and onions together. Remove from the pan. Saute Brussels sprouts in remaining bacon fat and toss together bacon, onions and sprouts. Season to taste.

Serves 4-6

Le Soufflé au Chocolat et Noix de Coco
Chocolate Coconut Souffle

60 gms (3 tablespoons) unsalted butter
60 gms (3 tablespoons) sugar
60 gms (3 tablespoons) flour
1½ cups milk
60 gms (3 tablespoons) sugar
¼ kg (½ lb) dark sweet chocolate
5 tablespoons grated coconut
4 egg yolks
6 egg whites
1 tablespoon butter for greasing dish.

Butter the inside of a souffle dish. Sprinkle sugar on the butter. Melt the chocolate in a pan over boiling water. Melt the butter in another saucepan and stir in the flour. Add the milk and sugar and bring to a boil, stirring continuously until the mixture thickens. Add the melted chocolate and coconut. Cool and fold in egg yolks. Mix well. Finally, beat egg whites until thick and stiff. Fold into chocolate mixture. Pour into souffle dish to fill ⅔ full. Bake for 20-25 minutes in 375° oven. Serve immediately with plenty of whipped cream.

Serves 4-6

La Mousse au Moka
Coffee Mousse

2¼ cups milk
4 egg yolks
2½ tablespoons sugar
2 tablespoons instant coffee powder
1¼ cup double cream, whipped
3 egg whites, beaten until stiff
¼ cup Mt. Kenya coffee liqueur
  (or any coffee liqueur)

Bring the milk to a boil in a saucepan. Combine egg yolks, sugar and coffee powder in another saucepan, and pour hot milk over the mixture, stirring continuously. Return to the stove and cook over very low heat without boiling, until the mixture coats the back of a spoon. Refrigerate until cold. Fold in the whipped cream. Fold in beaten egg whites. Stir in coffee liqueur. Pour into tall glasses and swirl with chocolate sauce if desired. Refrigerate 1 hour before serving. Garnish with whipped cream.

Serves 6

La Mangue Flambé à la Sinbad

Mango Flambé a la Sinbad

2 medium ripe mangos
2 tablespoons butter
2 tablespoons sugar
juice of 1 orange
¼ cup mango juice (tinned)
¼ cup Grand Marnier
1 cup double cream (slightly whipped)

Cut the mangos in half, and remove the seed. Peel, and cut fresh into ½-inch cubes. Pre-heat a frying pan. Toss in butter and add sugar, mixing with a wooden spoon for 30 seconds. Add juices and simmer before adding Grand Marnier. Flame, then reduce the liquid by ⅓ before adding mangos. Remove from the heat and allow to cool for a few minutes before gently folding in the semi-whipped cream.

Serves 4

La Délice aux Fraises

Delicious Strawberries

3 cups strawberries
1 cup strawberry yoghurt
½ cup double cream
60 gms (½ cup) sugar

Wash, remove tops of strawberries and rewash. Whip the cream, adding the sugar. Mix together with yoghurt and strawberries. Pile into individual glasses and garnish with whipped cream.

Serves 4

Les Oranges en Glace à la façon du Chef

Oranges served in Iced Coupes, Chef's Style

4 medium oranges
4 scoops vanilla ice cream
¼ cup Benedictine liqueur
¾ cup double cream
grated chocolate or cherries for garnish

Cut the tops off unpeeled oranges. Remove the fruit, keeping the cases intact. Place a scoop of ice cream in the case and decorate with orange segments. Pour on Benedictine liqueur and decorate with whipped cream and grated chocolate. To serve, place crushed ice in a glass coupe and rest the orange on top.

Serves 4

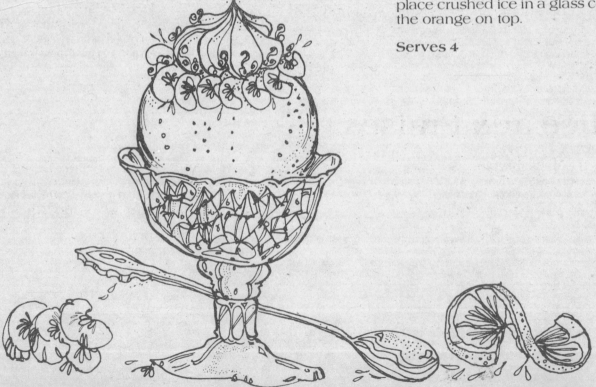

Traditional Cooking

JICHO NDIYO UFANYA
KAZI KUBWA KULIKO TUMBO

Traditional Cooking

Traditional Kenyan cooking provides a reflection of the many life-styles of the different peoples in the country. The nomadic Maasai eat simply, relying on the by-products of their cows and goats. They carry gourds filled with a junket-like mixture of cow's blood, fermented milk and urine and puzzle nutritionists by their excellent health, despite a total lack of vitamin C.

Contrasting to the spartan fare of the Maasai is the diet of the agrarian Kikuyu, who grow beans, maize and peas, which they cook and mash together to make *irio*. They roll *irio* into balls and dip them into meat or vegetables stews. Most people in Kenya make *ugali* their staple food. *Ugali*, or posho, is a maize meal porridge which is often served with *sukuma wiki*, a tasty dish prepared with greens and flavoured with left-over meats and other vegetables.

In the west of Kenya the people living by Lake Victoria make delicious stews from fresh lake fish, or dry the fish for transporting. These people prefer rice to *ugali*, as do the coastal peoples who enjoy the most varied diet of all. Their particular brand of "Swahili" cooking shows the influence of the traders and explorers who, over the centuries, have introduced new foods and spices to Kenya. The Arab culture can be most clearly seen on the tiny island of Lamu, where street sellers serve spicy cups of black coffee and sweetmeats, and the air is heavy with the smell of fish curries.

Although the recipes in this section give just a sampling of the food found in Kenya, for a true taste it is necessary to visit a home, and enjoy the delicious food for oneself.

Main dishes
Roast Chicken with Peanut Sauce
Stuffed Matura and Mahu
Nyanza Lamb Stew
Luo Dried Fish
Pumpkin Leaves in Peanut Butter
Swahili Seafish
Western Kenya Cabbage and Eggs

Accompaniments
Ugali
Fried Sweet Potatoes with Tomatoes
Cassava baked with Corn and Peanuts
Irio
Mseto
Ndizi
Meat with Banana Puree
Sukuma Wiki
Fried Locusts

Sweet Dishes
Sweet Potato and Coconut Dessert
Crunchy Matoke
Sesame Sweet Potato Balls

Roast Chicken with Peanut Sauce
Absolutely delicious with sweet potatoes or rice

Roast Chicken

1½ kilos (3 lbs) chicken
2 tablespoons butter or margarine for
  basting
salt and pepper.

Place the chicken in a roasting pan. Smear with margarine and season. Bake at 325° (no 3) for 2 hours, basting with juices.

Serves 4

Peanut Sauce

1 cup skinned peanuts (or substitute ½ cup crunchy peanut butter)
2 tablespoons margarine, butter or ghee
1 tomato, chopped
1 onion, chopped
1 cup milk
½ teaspoon salt

Place peanuts in a blender or food mincer, and reduce to a fine paste. In a frying pan, melt the ghee or margarine and fry the onions until barely golden. Stir in the chopped tomatoes and cook together five minutes. Add the peanut paste or peanut butter and blend well. Stir in the milk and salt. Cover the pan and allow to simmer 20-30 minutes. Stir occasionally.

Makes 1 cup.

Stuffed Mutura and Mahu

Beef-Stuffed Tripe

3 tablespoons chopped onions
½ teaspoon chopped garlic
1 tablespoon oil
¾ kg (1½ lbs) boneless forequarter
   of beef
1 green chilli, chopped
salt and pepper
1 tripe, approx. 200 gms (½ lb)
1 cup blood

Cook onions and garlic in oil until onions are golden brown. Cool. Cut the beef into small cubes. Mix with blood and season with salt, pepper and chilli. Place mixture in uncooked tripe and tie both ends firmly. Grill. Slice to serve. Traditionally this is served with *ugali* or *githeri*.

Serves 6

Nyanza Lamb Stew

4 tablespoons ghee or clarified butter
600 gms (1¼ lb) boneless shoulder
   of lamb, cubed
salt and pepper
2 onions, sliced
3 cloves garlic, chopped
4 tomatoes, chopped and seeded
2 teaspoons ginger, chopped
1 tablespoon finely chopped chillies
300 gms (½ lb) pumpkin, peeled and
   cubed
¾ cup water

In a thick saucepan, melt 2 tablespoons of ghee. Add lamb cubes seasoned with salt and pepper. Brown the lamb. Remove and keep warm. Saute the onions, garlic, ginger, chillies and tomatoes in remaining ghee for 6-8 minutes. Stir in lamb and pumpkin. Cook for 25 minutes, stirring occasionally to keep from burning. Pour on water, cover and cook for 40 minutes, or until the lamb is tender and the pumpkin turns into a puree. Season to taste and serve with *irio, ugali,* or *ndizi.*

Serves 6

Luo Dried Fish Stew (Omena)

Tiny dried fish resembling whitebait are necessary for this recipe

3 cups dried fish (*omena*)
4 cups water
½ cup cooking oil
½ kilo (1 lb) tomatoes
2 large onions, chopped
salt to taste
2 cups milk

Wash the fish in cold water. Place in a pan and simmer gently in 4 cups of water until the water is nearly evaporated. Drop the tomatoes into boiling water, and peel. Chop the tomatoes. In a frying pan, heat the oil. Stir in onions and tomatoes and cook gently until soft. Add the cooked fish and salt. Stir gently, taking care not to crush the fish. Add the milk and simmer about 30 minutes. The milk forms the gravy (*mchuzi*). Serve with *ugali* or rice.

Serves 4-6

Pumpkin Leaf in Peanut Butter

Substitute spinach for pumpkin leaves in this high protein, inexpensive dish

2 bunches of pumpkin leaf (½ kilo, 1 lb)
2 cups water
½ teaspoon baking soda
2 onions, chopped
3 medium tomatoes, chopped
½ cup lard or margarine
salt
1 cup milk
1 cup peanut butter

Remove rough stems and veins of the leaves. Wash the leaves and cut up finely. Place 2 cups of water in a pan and add ½ teaspoon soda. Bring to the boil and add the leaves. Cover and cook about 15 minutes. Cook onions and tomatoes in the cooking fat. When they are soft, add the cooked pumpkin leaves and stir together. Add salt, milk and peanut butter. Cook for about 15 minutes on a low heat, stirring so the vegetables do not stick to the pan. Serve with *ugali* or chapatis.

Serves 4-6

Swahili Seafish

1 whole fresh seafish (2 kg or 4 lbs)
2 tablespoons butter
1 tablespoon chopped garlic
1 onion, chopped
1 teaspoon turmeric
1 teaspoon cumin
½ teaspoon saffron
3 tomatoes, chopped
3 cups coconut milk (see guide)

Cut the fish into 6 equal portions. Melt the butter in a large pan and add the garlic and onions. Stir and fry quickly and add spices to coat the onions. Saute the fish with the garlic, onions, spices and tomatoes. Stir in coconut milk and allow to simmer for 10 minutes. Before serving, add 1 red-hot piece of charcoal (optional!) This enhances the taste of the sauce but leaves behind pieces of charcoal.

Serves 4

Western Kenya Cabbage and Egg

1 cup water
1 small cabbage, chopped
½ cup cooking oil or margarine
2 onions, chopped
2 large tomatoes, chopped
3-4 eggs
salt to taste

In a saucepan, boil one cup of water. Add the cabbage to the boiling water. Cover and cook for 10 minutes. Heat oil or margarine in a frying pan and add the onions and tomatoes. Cook gently until soft. Add the cabbage and salt and cook for another 10 minutes, stirring occasionally. Beat the eggs in a small bowl. Stir into the cabbage and cook for 3 minutes until set. Serve with rice, *ugali* or potatoes.

Serves 4—6

Ugali
The traditional Kenyan accompaniment to meats and stews

2 cups maizemeal (corn meal)
4 cups water
salt and pepper to taste

In a large saucepan, boil the water. Sprinkle maizemeal into boiling water, stirring. Cook porridge for 20 minutes until it is very thick and smooth. Stir continuously to keep the mixture from sticking or burning. Cover the pot and leave on a very low heat for 10-15 more minutes to finish the cooking. Season to taste.

Serves 6

Fried Sweet Potatoes with Tomatoes

3 medium sweet potatoes
3 tablespoons margarine
4 tomatoes
salt, pepper and chilli powder to taste

Peel sweet potatoes. Boil 30-40 minutes until soft. Peel and slice tomatoes. When the sweet potatoes have cooled, slice them into ⅛ inch pieces. In a large frying pan, melt the margarine. Fry the sweet potatoes until golden brown. Stir in chilli powder, salt and pepper. Add the tomatoes and cook 5 minutes more.

Serves 6

Cassava Baked with Corn and Peanuts

This delicate dish goes well with roast meats

1 cassava
1 ear of corn
6 tablespoons margarine
3 eggs
1 cup milk
4 tablespoons roasted peanuts
salt and pepper

In a heavy saucepan, boil the cassava until tender about 30 minutes. Slice thinly and put aside. Roast or grill the ear of corn, and remove kernels from the cob. In a frying pan, melt the margarine and stir in corn and chopped peanuts. Cook together for 2 minutes. Grease a 9-inch baking dish. Place a layer of sliced cassava on the bottom and cover with peanuts and corn. In a separate bowl, beat eggs until fluffy, add the milk and seasonings. Pour over the cassava. Bake in 350° oven for 20-25 minutes, until bubbling and set.

Serves 4

Irio

4 green corn cobs
400 gms (1 lb) beans
4 potatoes
½ kg (1 lb) spinach
salt and pepper

Boil the corn. Cut the kernels off the green corn cob. Boil the corn with the beans until soft. Peel and wash the potatoes and add to the corn and beans along with the chopped spinach. Boil together until the potatoes are soft. Season with salt and pepper, and mash.

Serves 6

Mseto

250 gms (1 cup) lentils
250 gms (1 cup) rice
1 onion, sliced
½ cup oil
1 cup milk
1 cup grated coconut
salt and pepper

Soak the lentils overnight in cold water. Discard this water and cover the lentils with fresh water before boiling until tender. Cook the rice and drain. Fry the onion in 2 tablespoons of oil. When lentils and rice are cooked, place in one large saucepan and add onions, coconut and milk. Cook gently to evaporate most of the liquid. Season with salt and pepper. This dish goes well with fish, meat or stewed chicken.

Serves 8

Ndizi
Spicy Matoke

8 plantain bananas (*matoke*)
juice of 1 lemon
1 tablespoon ghee or butter
2 onions, sliced
½ bunch fresh coriander leaves
1 whole chilli
2 cups beef stock

Peel the bananas and soak in lukewarm water with juice of one lemon for 2 minutes. Melt ghee in a large saucepan. Fry onions, chilli and coriander in ghee for 3 minutes. Add bananas and cover with 2 cups beef stock. Simmer for 30-35 minutes.
Serves 6

Meat with Banana Puree

750 gms (1 ½ lbs) stewing meat
6 small bananas
4 tablespoons chopped onions
2 tablespoons butter
2 cups, potatoes, chopped
salt and pepper
½ cup grated coconut (optional)

Cube the beef and place in a pan of cold water. Boil until tender. Peel the bananas and add to meat with the chopped onions. Cover and simmer until tender. Remove the meat. Add the butter to the bananas, mashing or liquidizing. The consistency of the finished puree should be like a heavy cream. Reheat the puree, season and serve separately with the meat. If you use coconut, add to the banana puree just before serving.
Serves 6

Sukuma Wiki

Sukuma Wiki means "push the week," and is the dish traditionally served frequently before pay day! It is infinitely variable and depends on what's in the house

½ kg (1 lb) Sukuma Wiki (Kale or Spinach)
1-2 chopped onions
2-4 chopped tomatoes
leftover meats
green pepper
2-3 tablespoons oil
salt and pepper

In a large frying pan, fry the onions until soft. Add tomatoes and green pepper, and any pieces of meat handy. Cook together until well-heated. Add cooked, chopped spinach and cook over low heat for 20-30 minutes until the mixture is well blended. Season to taste.

Serves 4

Fried Locusts

An acquired taste

2 cups young locusts
1 cup water
½ cup ghee or butter
salt and pepper

Strip wings and legs from the locusts. Place in a saucepan and simmer in the salted water until soft. Drain. Add ¼ cup of ghee. Fry until locusts become crisp. Add ¼ cup ghee and cook for 5 minutes.

Serves 4

Sweet Potato and Coconut Dessert
Like American pumpkin pie, without the crust

1½ cups sweet potatoes, boiled and
  mashed
1 cup grated coconut
¾ cup sugar
2 eggs
½ cup water
4 tablespoons butter, melted
½ teaspoon mixed spices
½ teaspoon cinnamon
1 cup milk

In a large bowl, beat sweet potatoes, coconut and sugar together until light. Stir in milk, water and butter. In another bowl, beat the eggs slightly, and stir into the mixture of sweet potatoes and milk. Add the spices and beat until very smooth. Put into a greased pie tin and bake for 30 minutes in 375° oven. Serve hot or cold.

Serves 4

Crunchy Matoke

8 *matoke* (plantains or green bananas)
½ cup margarine, melted
½ cup chopped peanuts
salt and pepper to taste

Steam matoke in a large saucepan until tender. Drain and roll in margarine. Roll each matoke in peanuts and season, before baking on a baking tray in 350° oven for 15 minutes.

Serves 8

Sesame Sweet Potato Balls

A very unusual sweet!

6 large sweet potatoes
8 tablespoons sugar
1 egg
1 cup sesame seeds
½ cup flour
oil for frying

In a large saucepan, place 2 cups of water. Bring to a boil and add the sweet potatoes. Steam until soft. Drain them, peel and mash them. When they have cooled, add sugar and egg and roll into 2-inch balls. Mix together ½ cup of flour and a little water to make a soft batter. Add the sesame seeds. Roll balls in the batter before deep frying in hot oil. Drain and serve.

Serves 6

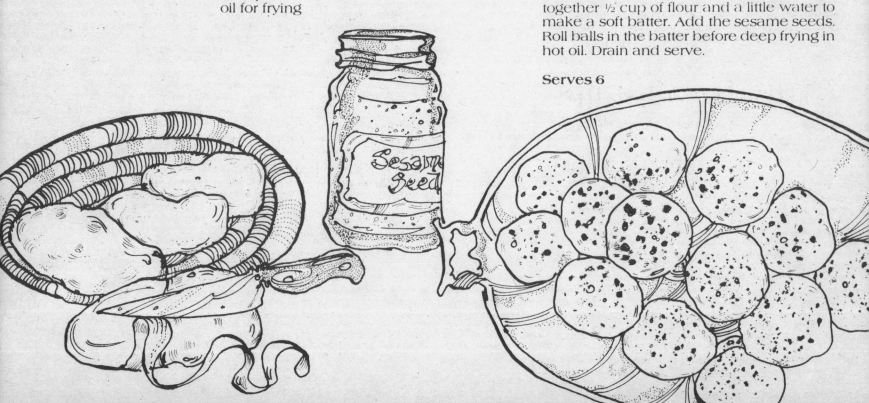

Curry Lunch

Curry Lunch

A Kenyan cookbook which devotes a section to Indian recipes may sound an odd idea to those who do not realize the Indian influence in Kenya. Early traders introduced exotic spices and new foods to Africa, while the influx of Indian workers led to the gradual awakening of interest in their strange cooking. The coastal people were the first to adapt the ideas to ingredients they found available in their area, but over the years, cooks all over the country learned how to make basic curries. The Sunday curry lunch became an institution, and now hotels and restaurants have their own special curry buffets with long tables filled with vegetable dishes, assorted curries, condiments and brightly coloured sweets.

Indian restaurants are now popular in the larger cities, providing unusual food at reasonable prices. The restaurants each have their own specialities, with Gujaratis concentrating on vegetable dishes, Punjabis serving their highly spiced fare, while Goans prepare a subtle blend of Portuguese and Indian cuisine.

The recipes in this chapter represent a typical curry lunch as prepared by hotels in Kenya. To recreate an Indian meal at home, choose one or two curries, a variety of condiments, and prepare a large bowl of rice or chapatis. Ideally, the dishes should be kept hot on a warming tray so guests can fill up their plates as often as they wish. Cold beer, or *lassi*, a refreshing yoghurt drink, make the ideal accompaniment for spicy curries, and the best dessert for most meals is something light and fruity.

Curries

Hyderabad Chicken Curry
Kashmiri Mutton
Pork Vindaloo
Madras Fish Curry
Kebab Curry
Palak Chicken

Accompaniments

Mixed Vegetable Raita
Sambhar
Tomato Raita
Gobi Sabji
Chapatis

Sweets

Lassi
Baked Mango and Rice
Carrot Halva
Banana Halva

Hyderabad Chicken Curry

1 chicken, cut into portions
1½ cups yoghurt
3 cloves garlic, crushed
1 teaspoon chopped fresh ginger
1½ teaspoons saffron (or turmeric)
2-3 green chillies, chopped
1 tablespoon caraway seeds
10 cardamoms
6 peppercorns
5 cm. (¾") stick cinnamon
4 cloves
1 teaspoon salt
1 teaspoon garam masala
3 tablespoons ghee or cooking oil
2 onions, sliced
3 tablespoons grated coconut
1 cup water of stock
juice of 1 lemon
handful of coriander leaves for garnish

Mix together the yoghurt, garlic, ginger and saffron in a large bowl. Place the chicken in the mixture and marinate for 2 hours. Grind the chillies, caraway seeds, cardamoms, peppercorns, cinnamon, cloves, salt and garam masala together to form a paste. Put aside. Heat the oil or ghee in a large frying pan until hot, and saute the onions slowly until golden brown. Add the ground spices and fry for 2 minutes. Add the chicken pieces, coconut and marinade and simmer. Stir in water or stock, and cook gently until tender. Add the lemon juice and place in a large serving dish. Garnish with coriander leaves before serving.

Serves 4

Kashmiri Mutton
The addition of the nuts to the dish is a Kenyan touch

1 kg (2 lbs) mutton or lamb, cubed
2-4 cardamoms
1 teaspoon chopped ginger
5 cm (¾ inch) cinnamon
1 teaspoon fennel seeds
4 cloves
6 peppercorns
6-7 cloves garlic
1½ teaspoons chilli powder
2-3 cups yoghurt
½ teaspoon saffron
1 tablespoon lemon juice
4 tablespoons ghee, oil or butter
½ cup almonds, blanched and chopped
½ cup cashewnuts, chopped

Grind together the spices. Put yoghurt in a large bowl and stir in the spices. Place lamb or mutton cubes in the yoghurt and marinate 1-2 hours. Stir the saffron into the lemon juice. Place the marinated meat in a large saucepan and simmer gently in the marinade until the liquid evaporates and the meat is tender, approximately 2 hours. Pour lemon juice and ghee over the meat and fry until brown. Saute the nuts separately, and sprinkle over the meat before serving with chapatis.

Serves 8

Pork Vindaloo
A classic dish from western India

2 tablespoons coriander seed
1 tablespoon cumin seeds
2 cardamons
3 cm. (1 inch) piece cinnamon
6 cloves
6 peppercorns
2 teaspoons turmeric
1 teaspoon chopped fresh ginger
1-2 teaspoons chilli powder
1 teaspoon salt
1 kg (2 lbs) pork cubes
2½ cups vinegar
2 bay leaves
1 tablespoon ghee or oil
6 cloves garlic, chopped
1 tablespoon ghee or oil
2 teaspoons mustard seeds

In a hot frying pan, lightly brown the coriander and cumin seeds. Grind or crush together with the rest of the spices to form a paste, to which you add a teaspoon of vinegar. Put aside. Dilute ½ cup of vinegar with ½ cup of water and wash the pork in the mixture. Drain and coat the meat with the spice paste. Sprinkle with broken bay leaves and pour the 2 cups of vinegar over the meat, and allow to marinate overnight. The next day, fry the chopped garlic in ghee or oil for a minute and add the mustard seeds. Fry for a few minutes. Add the meat and marinade, and simmer gently about 1½ hours until tender. This dish can be served hot or cold.

Serves 6

Madras Fish Curry

Marinade

    2 tablespoons vinegar
    1 tablespoon prepared chilli sauce
    1 teaspoon salt

Madras Fish Curry Marinade

    ½ teaspoon cumin seeds
    ½ teaspoon mustard seeds
    1 green chilli
    ½ teaspoon paprika
    ½ kg. (1 lb) fish fillets
    ½ teaspoon turmeric powder
    1 onion, sliced
    ½ cup water
    juice of 2 lemons
    2 tablespoons ghee for frying
    salt to taste

In a flat dish, place the fish fillets. Mix together the marinade ingredients and pour over the fish. Marinate at least 2-3 hours. Grind or blend together cumin, mustard, chilli, paprika and turmeric. Heat ghee or oil in a frying pan and saute fish, onions and spices together until the onions and fish are coated with spices. Add the lemon juice, water and salt and cook until tender.

Serves 4

Kebab Curry

For convenience, this recipe uses curry powder. Make sure it is fresh!

450 gms (1 lb) beef, mutton or veal
6 cm (3 inches) fresh ginger
4 onions, quartered
2-3 cloves garlic, chopped
1 tablespoon curry powder
½ teaspoon garam masala
½ teaspoon cumin
3-5 green chillies
1 cup beef stock or hot water
5-6 tomatoes, peeled and quartered
handful fresh coriander leaves

Cut the meat into cubes. Peel and slice the ginger into pieces which can be threaded on to a skewer. Thread the meat, quartered onions and ginger on 4 skewers. In a frying pan, heat the butter or oil and stir in any remaining onions and chopped garlic. Add curry powder, garam masala, cumin and finely chopped chillies. Fry for 3 minutes. Add the skewers, the stock and tomatoes. Simmer about 1 hour until the meat is tender. Serve the skewers sprinkled with coriander leaves.

Serves 4

Palak Chicken

This delicious recipe is easy to prepare and beautiful to serve

1 large chicken
3 tablespoons ghee or clarified butter
2 onions, sliced
4-5 cloves garlic, chopped
4 cm (1½ inch) fresh ginger, chopped
3 cm (1¼ inch) stick cinnamon
4-5 cardamoms
2 teaspoons coriander powder
½ kg (1 lb) fresh spinach
4-5 chopped tomatoes, peeled
2-3 green chillies

In a large frying pan heat the ghee or clarified butter. Add the onions and saute until golden brown. Grind or blend together the spices and stir into the onions, coating them with the spices. Add the chicken and lightly brown. Add chopped spinach, peeled tomatoes and chillies. Cover and cook over low heat about 1 hour until the meat is tender.

Serves 4

Mixed Vegetable Raita
A perfect contrast to the spicy curries

2 cups yoghurt
½ teaspoon salt
½ cup cucumber, chopped
1 tomato, chopped
1 onion, chopped
1 green chilli, chopped
pinch cumin
pinch black pepper
2 tablespoons coriander leaves,
  chopped

Beat the yoghurt and salt together. Add the chopped vegetables. Sprinkle with cumin and black pepper, and garnish with coriander leaves. Chill before serving.

Makes 2 cups

Sambhar
This lentil vegetable dish provides a visual contrast to the curries

1 cup lentils
2 carrots, chopped
2 potatoes chopped
1½ teaspoon salt
2 teaspoons turmeric powder
3 cups water
2 tablespoons ghee or clarified butter
1 teaspoon cumin
2 teaspoons coriander
1½ tablespoons mustard seeds
2 green chillies, chopped
2 teaspoons garam masala
1 teaspoon curry powder
juice of 1 lemon

Wash and soak the lentils overnight. Boil with carrots, potatoes, turmeric powder and salt in 3 cups of water until soft. Melt ghee in a frying pan. Fry the coriander, and cumin, gradually adding the mustard seeds, chillies and a pinch of curry powder. Add the garam masala and stir well. Serve hot, adding lemon juice just before serving.

Serves 4

Tomato Raita

½ kg (1 lb) ripe tomatoes, chopped and
  peeled
1 cup shredded coconut
2 tablespoons green chillies, minced
½ teaspoon salt
2 cups yoghurt
1 tablespoon oil
1½ teaspoons whole mustard seeds
½ teaspoon dried red pepper, crushed

Combine coconut and tomatoes in a bowl. Add chillies, salt and yoghurt and mix together. In a small frying pan, heat the oil. Fry the mustard seeds and red pepper in it until the seeds begin to pop. Pour into yoghurt mixture and stir in quickly. Chill before serving.

Makes 2½ cups

Gobi Sabji
This cabbage dish can be varied by adding a tablespoon of coconut if desired

2 tablespoons oil or clarified butter
2 onions, finely chopped
½ teaspoon whole mustard seeds
2 tomatoes, peeled and chopped
1 small cabbage, finely chopped
2 green chillies, chopped
¼ teaspoon turmeric powder
1 teaspoon salt

Heat oil or butter in a frying pan. Add onions, mustard seeds and tomatoes, and cook for 10 minutes. Stir in cabbage, chillies and turmeric, and cover the pan, cooking ½ hour or until the cabbage is tender. Add salt to taste. You may add a tablespoon of coconut, but do not add any water.

Serves 4

Chapatis

This simple bread often takes the place of rice in an Indian meal

2 cups flour
½ teaspoon salt
½ cup water
clarified butter or ghee for brushing
   on chapatis

Stir together salt and flour. Stir in water and knead with fingers until the dough is elastic, approximately 5 minutes. Divide into 12 pieces. Roll each piece into a ball. Use a rolling pin to roll out into thin circles on a floured cloth. Each circle should be approximately 7 inches across. Heat an ungreased frying pan. Cook the chapatis on one side until they puff up and brown spots appear. Turn over and cook the other side. Stack chapatis on a plate, brushing each one with ghee.

Makes 12 chapatis

Lassi
A cooling drink which goes perfectly with spicy foods

1 glass cold water
2 tablespoons yoghurt
1 tablespoon lemon juice
dash of salt
sugar to taste

Stir the yoghurt into a glass of water. Add lemon juice, salt and sugar. Fill the glass with ice cubes.

Makes 1 serving

Baked Mango and Rice
A delicate sweet which can be served hot or chilled

½ kilo (1 lb) rice
½ cup sugar
1 cup milk
½ kilo (1 lb) sweet mango puree
1 cup double cream
½ teaspoon ground saffron
2 teaspoons rose water

Soak rice overnight. Boil the milk until reduced by half. Mix the mango puree, cream and boiled milk in a bowl, then add sugar, saffron and rose water. Boil the rice until very soft. Put a layer in a deep dish and top with a layer of creamed mango. Repeat. Dot with a little butter and place in a slow oven until set and lightly browned.

Serves 8

Carrot Halva
A very sweet dessert

¾ kg (1½ lbs) carrots
8 cups milk
½ inch stick cinnamon
3 cardamom seeds
¼ cup raisins
¼ cup butter
2 tablespoons honey
¾ cup sugar
¼ cup blanched almonds
½ teaspoon rose water (optional)

Grate the carrots and set aside with the juice. In a saucepan, scald the milk and add carrots and cinnamon. Boil for 1 minute. Simmer and stir often over low heat. When the milk has been reduced to less than a quarter, stir in the cardamoms, saffron (dissolved in 1 tablespoon boiling water) and the raisins. Mix and stir until the milk is dry. Enrich with the butter and stir over a medium heat until the milk has been absorbed and coats mixture. Add honey and sugar. Stir and cook for 8 minutes more until a rich translucent red. Add slivered or halved almonds, and water if desired. It may be served chilled with cream.

Serves 8

Banana Halva

6 large ripe bananas
¼ cup butter
1 cup water
¼ cup sugar
Pinch of nutmeg
1 **ground cardamom**
a little almond essence
2 tablespoons blanched slivered almonds

Peel and slice the bananas in 1 inch pieces, and fry in butter in a frying pan for 7 minutes, stirring frequently. Remove and mash. Add 5 tablespoons of water and simmer on a low heat, stirring constantly for 3 minutes. Dissolve sugar in remaining water and add to the banana puree. Boil together for 10 to 12 minutes, stirring to keep the mixture from burning. Cook until thick, and turn into a bowl. Whisk until smooth and light. Sprinkle **with nutmeg, cardamom and almonds. Chill before serving.**

Serves 6

Comparative Measures and Ingredients Guide

The cups and tablespoons quoted in this book are the American standards, which are slightly smaller in capacity than British standard cups and spoons. The American standard ½ pint measuring cup has a capacity of 8 fluid ounces; the British ½ pint has a capacity of 10 fluid ounces. A standard-sized teacup can be used for the recipes in *Tastes of Kenya*, as the addition or subtraction of a few ounces here or there doesn't usually make an enormous difference in a recipe.

Liquid Measures

Continental	American
1 litre	4½ cups
1 demilitre	2 cups
1 decilitre	½ cup

Weight

Continental	American
1 gram	035 ounce
100 grams	3½ ounces
500 grams	1 lb
1 kilogram	2¼ lbs

Coconut milk is easily made by placing one cup of chopped coconut flesh in an electric blender, and adding one cup of hot water. Blend at high speed for a minute or two until the coconut is reduced to a smooth puree. Grated coconut can also be used. Simply pour 1 cup of boiling water over the grated coconut and allow it to sit. Strain the coconut and use the "milk" in recipes requiring it.

Chillies must be handled with care. After cutting them, do not rub your eyes! Store them in the refrigerator, as they lose their flavour quickly.

Coriander leaves are often specified in the recipes. Buy coriander in bunches and keep refrigerated.

Curry Powder is usually not used in East African cooking, except as a convenient substitute for grinding the spices at home. Curry powder must be fresh!

Ginger Root is traditionally used by the Asian community in Kenya in preference to ground ginger powder. However, if ginger root is not available, substitute half the quantity of ginger powder.

Plantains or *matoke* are similar to bananas in appearance, but must be cooked before being eaten.

Mount Kenya Liqueur is the Kenyan equivalent of a coffee liqueur.

Sour milk can be made from fresh milk by adding 1 tablespoon of vinegar to a scant cup of milk and stirring.

Aioli 24
Avocados
  Chef's Style 36
  Kaimosi with Hot Dressing 26
  Guacamole 27

Baked Red Mullet with Honey 8
Bananas
  Cheese Cake 15
  Halva 73
  Meat with Banana Puree 57
  Ndizi 57
Barbecued Chicken 22
Barbecued Spare Ribs 21
Bearnaise Sauce 23
Beef
  Fillet of all Seasons 40
  Gourmandise Brillat Savarin 39
  Grilled Laikipia Rump Steak 22
  Kebab Curry 68
  Stuffed Mutura and Tripe 51
Brocoli Polonaise (with Hard Boiled
  Egg) 43
Brussels Sprouts sauteed with Bacon and
  Onions 42
Butter
  Madras 23
  Maitre d'hôtel 24

Cake
  Banana Cheese 15
  Hot Mango Delight 31
Canard Rôti aux Mangues 39
Carrè d'agneau Roti Provençale 41
Carrot
  and Courgettes Salad 28

Halva 73
Cassava baked with Corn and
  Peanuts 55
Chapatis 71
Chicken
  Barbecued 22
  Hyderabad Curry 64
  Palak 68
  Roast with Peanut Sauce 50
  Skewered with Saffron 20
Chocolate
  Coconut Souffle 44
  Coconut Crust Pie 32
Choux de Bruxelles au Lard 43
Coastal Coconut Prawns 7
Cucumber
  Chilled Soup 6
  Sour Cream Salad 26
Coconut
  Coastal Prawns 7
  Crust Chocolate Pie 32
  Sweet Potato and 59
  Whole fresh Seafish stuffed with Coconut
    and Ginger 8
Crevettes au Beurre Froid 37
Curry Dressing 28
Curries
  Beef Kebab 68
  Hyderabad Chicken 64
  Kashmiri Mutton 65
  Madras Fish 67
Palak Chicken 68
  Pork Vindaloo 65

Desserts
  Baked Mango and Rice 72

Banana Cheese Cake 15
Banana Halva 73
Carrot Halva 73
Chocolate Souffle 44
Coconut Crust Chocolate Pie 32
Coffee Mousse 44
Crunchy Matoke 59
Hot Mango Delight 31
Lemon Milk Sorbet 31
Malindi Lime Mousse 14
Mango Flambé à la Sinbad 45
Oranges en Glace 46
Pineapples and Kirsch 14
Strawberries Délice 45
Super Strawberry Ice Cream 30
Taita Fruit Salad with Grand Marnier
  Sauce 16
Tropical Syllabub 15
Dilled Prawn Salad 11
Drinks
  Keekorok Claret Punch 30
  Nairobi Breeze 29
  Sangria 29
  Teaplanters Punch 29
  Toto Special 30
Duckling
  Roast with Mangos 39

Épinards a la Creme 42

Fillet de Porc Naivasha 38
Fish
  Baked Red Mullet with Honey 8
  Dilled Prawns 10
  Fillet with Cashewnuts 9
  Grilled Lobster Negresco 9

Fish (Continued)
Lobster Diable 10
Luo Dried Fish Stew 52
Madras Fish Curry 67
Omeno 52
Prawns en Brochette 10
Prawns in Cold Butter 37
Swahili Seafish 53
Whole Fresh Seafish stuffed with
  Coconut and Ginger 8
Fennel and Mushroom Salad 12
Fresh Spinach and Cheese Salad 11
Gazpacho Andalouse 6
Gobi Samji 70
Grand Marnier Sauce 16
Grilled Laikipia Rump Steak 22
Grilled Lobster Negresco 9
Gourmandise Brillat Savarin 39
Guacamole 27

Hollandaise Sauce 25
Hot Mango Delight 31
Hot Rice Salad 13

Ice Cream and Sorbets
  Lemon Milk Sorbet 31
  Oranges en Glace 40
  Super Strawberry Ice Cream 30
  Strawberry Delice 45
Irio 56

Kali Tomato Sauce 24
Kebabs
  Curry 68
  Molo Lamb with Paloise Butter 22
  Skewered Chicken with Saffron 20
Keekorok Claret Punch 30
Kenya Coffee Mousse 32

Kitale Pork Chops 20

Lamb/Mutton
  Kashmiri Mutton Curry 65
  Mango Stuffed 20
  Molo Kebabs with Paloise Butter 22
  Nyanza Lamb Stew 51
  Saddle Provencale 41
Lassi 72
Lemon Milk Sorbet 31
Lobster
  Diable 10
  Grilled Negresco 9
Locusts, fried 58
Luo Dried Fish Stew 52
Madras Butter 23
Madras Fish Curry 67
Maitre d'Hôtel Butter 24
Malindi Lime Mousse 14
Manges Tout au Beurre 42
Mangos
  Baked with Rice 72
  Hot Delight 31
  Flambe a la Sinbad 45
  Stuffed Shoulder of Lamb 21
  With Spicy Prawns 36
Mangues aux Crevettes Rosés 36
Mangues Flambé à la Sinbad 45
Matoke, Crunchy 59
Mayonnaise 25
Meat with Banana Puree 57
Melon with Sour Cream and Honey 37
Melon en Surprise 37
Mousse
  Coffee 44
  Kenya Coffee 32

Malindi Lime 14
Smoked Sailfish 38
Mousse de Voile de Poisson Fume 38
Msetso 56
Nairobi breeze 29
Ndizi 57
Norfolk Caesar Salad 13
Nyanza Lamb Stew 51
Omena 52
Oranges en Glace à la Façon du Chef 46
Palak Chicken 68
Paloise Sauce 22
Peanut Sauce 50
Pineapples and Kirsch 14
Pommes Caroline 42
Pork
  Barbecued Spareribs 21
  Fillet Naivasha 38
  Kitale Chops 20
  Vindaloo 65
Potatoes
  Fried Sweet Potatoes with Tomatoes 55
  Sesame Sweet Potato Balls 60
  Sweet Potatoes and Coconut 59
  With Chives and Tarragon 42
Prawns
  Coastal Coconut 7
  Dilled Salad 10
  En Brochettes 10
  In Cold Butter 37
Pumpkin Leaves in Peanut Butter 52

Ratatouille 27
Rice
  Baked Mango and 72
  Hot Salad 13

Salads
  Avocado Kaimosi with Hot Dressing 26
  Cucumber Sour Cream 26
  Curried Carrot and Courgette 28
  Dilled Prawn 10
  Fennel and Mushroom 12
  Gobi Sabji 70
  Guacamole 27
  Hot Rice 13
  Marinated Green Beans 12
  Norfolk Caesar Salad 13
  Ratatouille 27
  Sambhar 68
  Tomato Raita 70
  Vegetable Raita 69
Sangria 39
Sorbet (see Ice Creams)
Soufflé au Chocolat et Noix de Coco 44
Soups
  Chilled Cucumber 6
  Gazpacho 6
  Yoghurt 7
Spinach (or Kale)
  Fried Spinach and Cheese 11
  Sukuma Wiki 58
  With Fresh Cream 42
Strawberries
  Délice 45
  Super Ice Cream 30
Stuffed Mutura and Tripe 51
Sukuma Wiki 58
Swahili Seafish 53

Taita Fruit Salad with Grand Marnier
  Sauce 16
Teaplanter's Punch 29

Tomatoes
  Kali (Hot) Sauce 24
  Marinated 26
  Raita 70
Toto Special 30
Tourelle de Toutes Saisons 40
Tropical Syllabub 15
Veal Escalopes with Parmesan Sauce 39
Vegetables
  Baked Cassava with Corn and
  Peanuts 55
  Broccoli Polonaise 43
  Brussels Sprouts 42
  Fried Sweet Potatoes with Tomatoes 55
  Gobi Sabji 70
  Irio 56
  Mange Tout (Baby Pea Pods) 42
  Mseto 56
  Ndizi 57
  Pumpkin Leaves in Peanut Butter
    Sauce 52
  Sesame Sweet Potato Balls 60
  Spinach with Fresh Cream 42
  Sukuma Wiki 58

Western Kenya Cabbage and Egg 54
Whole Fresh Seafish stuffed with Coconut
  and Ginger 8

Yoghurt Soup 7